SLOTS!

How to Improve Your Odds

Andrew N.S. Glazer

Publications International, Ltd.

Andy Glazer is one of the most acclaimed gaming writers in the world. He is the author of *Casino Gambling the Smart Way*, and he writes a weekly gaming column for the *Detroit Free Press*. He is also a regular contributor to *Chance Magazine, Card Player Magazine, Midwest Gaming* and *Travel Magazine*, and *DoubleDown Magazine*. To contact Mr. Glazer, visit his Web site at www.Casinoselfdefense.com, or call 888-ODDS-WIN.

ISBN: 0-7853-4928-6

Contents

○ ○ ○ ○ ○

Spin Those Reels!

Slots dominate the modern casino scene because they are easy to play and offer the promise of big winnings for a small investment. Learn what kind of slot will likely satisfy you most, as well as strategies to increase your chances of winning more.

On the surface, slot machines seem to be the ultimate in passive gambling. You put your money in, pull a lever or push a button, and wait to see whether you win or lose. But the surface does not always reveal the entire story.

A knowledgeable slot player is far from passive. While it may not be possible to be a long-term winner at slots (unless you're extraordinarily lucky or a video poker expert), it is *very* possible to play much better than average. If you know what you're doing, you can reduce the house edge to the absolute minimum, learn how to avoid bad machines and classic mistakes, and put yourself in a position where you won't depend so much on luck to have a winning trip.

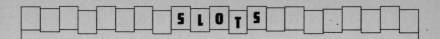

By learning how to approach playing slots, you'll also have more winning trips. If you do sometimes lose, you'll lose less, but when you win, you'll win more.

"That's not possible," you might say. "A slot machine is just a slot machine. All I can really do is cross my fingers. Where's the 'skill'? How can I 'learn' what I'm doing?"

All of those are reasonable questions, but they have answers, and you'll get them here. You won't need to memorize any complex tables or strategies. A lot of what's true about slot machines makes sense once you've heard it, so it won't be a problem to remember.

You'll learn about slot clubs and how their different features can make a big difference in the long run. You'll learn about the best places to play slots in all senses of the word: the best cities, the best casinos within a given city, and the best slots within a given casino.

You'll also learn what kind of slot is likely to give you the most enjoyment. Different kinds of slots behave very differently, and your motivation for playing is probably different from your neighbor's. This book discusses motivations and the machines that best suit each player.

In short, you'll learn some easy-to-remember facts, as well as some important questions to ask yourself. By the time you're done reading, it's likely your next trip to the casino will be more satisfying in every way.

CHAPTER ONE

Defining Your Mission

Most people play slots for some combination of entertainment, gambling thrill, and the money they can win. Depending on your goals, some slot machines will be better for you than others. There are few universal slot truths, and many plays that are right for one person are wrong for another.

The first question you should ask yourself is what, exactly, do you enjoy about playing slot machines? This isn't a trick question. Until you know why you like slots, you can't pick your best strategy. You want to maximize wins and minimize losses, but that demands different factors for different people. This strategy will determine the slots you'll want to play, how you'll want to play them, and how much money you'll want to put into play.

Different Machines for Different People

Let's look at a few examples. George might like playing slots because as he spins the reels, he loves to dream about

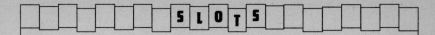

hitting a giant progressive jackpot that would change his life forever. Actually hitting this jackpot would be great, of course, but it's the dream, exciting and pleasant in its own right, that keeps George dropping the coins and spinning the reels.

Barbara, on the other hand, might like playing slots because she loves to hear that buzzer and see the flashing light that announces, "You win!" While she gets more excited about winning 1,000 coins than 10 coins, of course, the part that really floats her boat is that winning moment.

As you've already guessed, George and Barbara should be playing very different kinds of slot machines. There are slots well suited for each of them. George needs a progressive slot, where the jackpot keeps growing and growing. Barbara, however, prefers frequent jackpots, large or small. She's not going to wait patiently for that huge, but very rare, payoff.

But surely there are more than two choices. Let's take a look at some other playing styles.

Melissa loves the casino atmosphere. She can just feel the electricity in the air, and she enjoys watching all the people, getting free drinks, and talking to other players. She finds the chairs at the slot machines comfortable, and she likes to play eight to ten hours a day when she travels to a casino.

Charlie, on the other hand, looks for the thrill that comes from big action. He loves putting a lot of money at risk for a little while, feeling his heart pound, and then taking a breather to relive the experience and walk around.

Melissa and Charlie obviously have different playing styles, and they need different slot machines to accommodate them. On any given day, Melissa and Charlie can visit the same casino with the same expected mathematical result, but they won't both be happy on the same machine. They not only need to select different kinds of machines, they need to play them differently, as well.

Melissa wants to soak in the casino atmosphere, so she needs to find a slot that doesn't cost a lot to play—a low-denomination machine that accepts nickels or quarters. She should probably pull the handle rather than press a Spin Reels button, to slow the game down further.

Charlie, as we've seen, isn't going to be very happy at a quarter machine. He should be on a dollar machine playing maximum coins, or maybe even a $5 or $25 machine. Once he's found one of these higher-denomination machines, he should fire away at high speed for half an hour or so, and then go walk around town to take in the sights, secure and content in his "high roller" self-image. If he really wants to play the high roller, he can visit some casinos featuring machines that use special $1,000 tokens, but

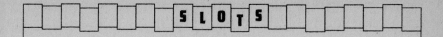

Charlie had better be pretty rich if he wants to play one of those!

I Want My Vacation Cheap!

Sometimes two players can even have exactly the same goal, such as taking advantage of the deals casinos offer, but still need to pursue it in very different ways. Steve, for example, is the King of Coupons. He loves those "fun books" that give you ten dollars in coins for only five dollars or a free roll of quarters after you've played for half an hour. He knows that, by taking advantage of promotional offers, he can get himself a pretty cheap vacation. He also likes the idea that he's beating the casino at its own game by grabbing the promotional dollars without hanging around long enough to lose a lot of money.

Marney, on the other hand, also wants freebies, but she's not satisfied with five dollars' worth of free coins. Marney wants the casino to give her a complimentary room and meals, called "comps"—and maybe some free luggage while they're at it.

Steve and Marney shouldn't go to Las Vegas together—they obviously need to take very different kinds of trips. Steve most enjoys moving from casino to casino, hitting every little promotional special. He'll end up visiting a number of casinos, eating free hot dogs and 99-cent

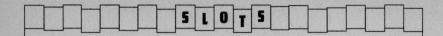

shrimp cocktails in different places. Marney, however, gets what she wants by joining a slot club and making sure that her slot-club card is inserted in every machine she plays. Most importantly, she needs to give all of her action to one casino. If she spreads her play out among ten different casinos, no one is going to comp anything for her. By staying in one place, she'll play enough hours a day at a high-enough-limit machine to reap a lot of slot club rewards, up to and possibly including the RFB (room, food, and beverage) comp that a lot of slot players think only table players can earn.

In the Zone

Many people go to casinos to get away or to escape, but there are a number of different ways a player can choose to escape. John, for example, likes to go into an almost zombielike trance, pushing buttons, spinning reels, and barely noticing what's happening around him, including what's happening on the machine. He enjoys what he might call "slot hypnosis."

Rachel also likes to escape, but she wants to take an active part in her entertainment. She enjoys seeing a game unfold, but she likes making decisions that can affect her outcome. She enjoys the feeling that she outwitted an opponent.

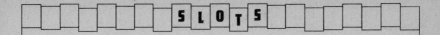

Frank shares some interests with Rachel, but Frank is a member of the TV generation, raised with a television set as his baby-sitter. He likes to watch amusing things happen on the screen in front of him.

As you may have guessed, John, Rachel, and Frank need to play very different kinds of machines, too. John needs a machine that is, no insult intended, idiot-proof. He wants to put the money in, push the button, and, as soon as something happens, push the button again. He has no need to think about anything that would detract from his escapist frame of mind.

Rachel would be bored by a machine like this because she wants to influence the outcome. She'd probably be happiest playing video poker, where she'll have to make a decision on every hand. If she wins, she'll feel like she earned it. If she loses, she can still walk away from the machine feeling like she played well but was just unlucky.

Frank didn't like slot machines much until about 1996, when a new breed of slot started to arrive. As the new millennium hit, Frank found that he'd come to love slot machines. He could sit and play *The Three Stooges, Let's Make a Deal, The Munsters,* or all sorts of other video slots that reminded him of his favorite shows. These new machines had special effects that let him enjoy two of his favorite pleasures simultaneously: gambling and watching TV.

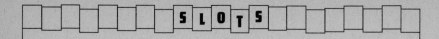

The Choice Is Yours

It should be obvious that there is no particular type of slot machine that is right for everyone, and there is no single right way to play the slots.

This chapter has focused on one part of the slot-playing equation, "as long as the hobby is fun." You've seen how your own personal preferences and personality traits can help you select the right kind of machine for you. Take a few minutes to pinpoint what you really enjoy about playing the slots, and from there you can figure out which machine will give you the most enjoyment. In the chapters that follow, you'll learn how to maximize your chances of winning on that machine.

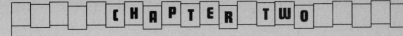

CHAPTER TWO

Types of Slot Machines

Slots come in all shapes and sizes, but it's what's inside that counts. In this chapter you'll discover how the construction of modern slots affects your play, how to eliminate some unhelpful slot myths, and how to select the right kind of machine.

O nce upon a time, slot machines were nonelectric mechanical devices not-so-affectionately called "one-armed bandits." The lever that spun the reels was the arm, of course. And the "bandit"? Well, these early machines didn't offer the player much of a chance.

About the only good thing you could say about these machines was that, if you were smart, you could figure out the odds against you. You could see the number of stops on each reel, and if you were good at math, you could "reckon" (this was the Wild West, after all) that with three reels, and 20 stops on each reel, the odds against hitting the big jackpot were 8,000-to-1 ($20 \times 20 \times 20 = 8,000$). This is, of course, assuming the machine was honest, which was

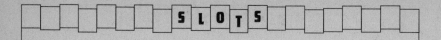
not necessarily a good assumption back then. Even if the machine were honest, though, the return on the big jackpot was likely nowhere close to 8,000-to-1.

Today's slot machines bear little resemblance to these ancestors. Unless the machine you are playing is very old (which nowadays you'll probably only find in an Eastern European country), you're almost certainly playing an electronic device whose heart is a computer chip called a Random Number Generator (RNG). We'll talk about what the RNG means to you soon, but first let's look at the different types of slot machines you'll find in the casino.

Slots are divided into two main categories, progressive and nonprogressive. There are also some important subgroups: multiplier/nonmultiplier and decision/no decision.

Progressive Slots

A progressive slot has a top (and sometimes a secondary) jackpot that varies. There is usually a meter right on top of the machine displaying both the jackpot and the speed at which it is growing.

All progressives work on the same principle. The machine has a basic starting point for the jackpot. The longer it continues without hitting the jackpot, the larger that jackpot grows. A percentage of each dollar played in the machine is held back and added to the jackpot. When someone hits the jackpot, the machine pays out and resets to the base jackpot level.

Some progressive machines are individual. The jackpot meter increases only when that specific machine is played. These jackpots tend to be small and to grow slowly. More common, however, is a single jackpot tied to a bank of perhaps 10 or 12 machines, with the communal jackpot increasing anytime anyone plays any of the machines.

Some slots, such as *Megabucks, Nevada Nickels,* or *Wheel of Fortune,* are "wide-area progressives." Thousands of these machines are linked together all over a state, so jackpots grow huge quickly. Of course, these are also the kinds of machines with the lowest odds of hitting that big jackpot.

When playing a progressive slot, it is vitally important to play it for the maximum number of coins. In virtually all cases, if you do not do this, you cannot win the big progressive jackpot, even if the right symbols come up on the machine. In that case, some machines will provide a small token payment, and others will provide absolutely nothing! We'll look at this situation more closely in Chapter 4.

Nonprogressive Slots

Nonprogressive slots usually feature jackpots expressed as a total number of coins printed right on the machine. You won't see a changing jackpot meter on these machines. A top

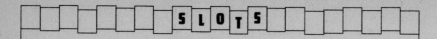

jackpot might be 1,000 or 10,000 coins, for example. It's important to remember that the jackpot is listed in *coins*, not dollars. If you are playing a nickel machine and hit a jackpot of 10,000 coins, you have just won 10,000 nickels, worth $500. While $500 is not to be sneezed at, it is not the life-changing sum that $10,000 can be.

Although the jackpot on a nonprogressive slot is fixed, it is usually important to play for maximum coins, unless the machine is a multiplier machine. On a multiplier, the top jackpot might be 1,000 coins if you play one coin, 2,000 coins if you play two, and 3,000 coins if you play three. There is no special bonus for playing the maximum: Your expected result is the same whether you play one coin at a time for three hours or three coins at a time for one hour.

The majority of nonprogressive slots, however, are not multiplier machines. It is fairly typical to see top jackpots of 1,000 for one coin, 2,000 for two coins, and 10,000 for three coins. We'll discuss this further in Chapter 4.

Decision Versus No-Decision Slots

Other than the choice of whether or not to play maximum coins, most slot machines don't require players to make decisions. You put your money in, push the button, and hope.

An increasingly large number of machines, however, are adding choices for the slot player. Video poker, one kind of decision machine, gets its own chapter later. But many other machines now give players a choice to try features that can double their bonuses or halve them, depending on various factors. In general, however, anytime a casino gives you the chance to make a decision, it's really giving you the chance to make a mistake. Choose poorly, and you can lose more quickly. For this reason, you should be careful when you consider playing a decision machine. The chance to participate in your fate can add fun, but it also adds risk.

What RNGs Mean for You

Now that we've seen different types of slots, let's return to something they all have in common. Remember the Random Number Generator, the computer chip at the heart of electronic slot machines? Information about how RNG chips operate will help you understand why machines pay as they do. It will also help you understand how many commonly held beliefs about slots are completely wrong. Knowing what's really happening in the machine will help you recognize what's really going on during your game.

An RNG is set at the chip factory to spit out millions of random number combinations every second. These combinations determine which symbols come up on the reels. As we've seen, an older reel with 20 symbols had 20 "stops," making it easy to calculate odds on hitting the jackpot.

Reels on today's machines, however, have "virtual" stops. A symbol that seems to come up one time in 20 might really come up only one time in 256. That changes the odds of hitting a top jackpot tremendously. The formula on older slots, 20 × 20 × 20, is only 8,000, making the odds 8,000-to-1 against hitting something that comes up only once on each reel. But when the numbers are 256 × 256 × 256, we get more than 16 million, which is quite another story. If you add a fourth reel with 256 stops, the odds against hitting The Big One move up to more than 4-billion-to-1!!!

Because the RNG is constantly spitting out these random combinations, you hit a big or small jackpot based on which millionth of a second you happen to pull the handle or hit the "spin reels" button. A jackpot isn't predestined to hit on, let's say, the 5,635th spin of the day.

The Slot Player's Nightmare That Isn't

The ultimate slot player's nightmare—and we've all had it—is to sit in front of a machine all day and, after hours and hours of play, finally move on to go to dinner. As soon as you leave the machine, another person comes along, puts three coins into it, and hits a mega-jackpot.

"If only I'd played one more minute!" you wail in the nightmare, thinking about your lost fortune and how unfair life is that another player can hit "your" jackpot.

But remember, it's only a nightmare. The real world doesn't work that way.

In this situation, the new player hit a jackpot because he happened to pull the lever at exactly the right millionth of a second. If you'd been at that same machine another minute, you likely wouldn't have pulled the lever at that same microsecond, and so you probably would not have won the jackpot. On an intellectual level at least, if this ever happens to you, you won't think you made the mistake of your life by getting up. Emotionally, of course, it still may be a bit hard to swallow, but at least now you can leave your machine at dinnertime with a bit more peace of mind.

Close-but-No-Cigar Isn't Really Close

Another effect of the RNG is that the combinations really are random: No patterns emerge, no matter what you think you're seeing. If a machine "just barely misses" a jackpot two or three times, don't think that the machine is "ready to hit" because it has been coming so close. One spin has absolutely nothing to do with the next one, just as one roll of the dice at a craps table has nothing to do with the next one. Of course, a lot of gamblers don't believe that dice rolls are random either, but if you don't believe that, you aren't going to be convinced that the same situation exists with slot machines. You need to take it on faith that in an

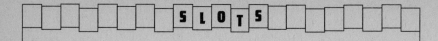

honest machine, there are no patterns you can spot. You just have to get lucky.

For the same reason, there's nothing physical you can do to a machine in the course of regular play to make it pay off. Jiggling handles, pulling it slowly or quickly, pressing the button instead of pulling the handle—none of these really matters. What does matter is picking the right millionth of a second, and humans can't do that on purpose.

"I've Consumed Too Many Coins, I Have to Give Some Back"

Another popular theory is that if you feed enough money into a machine, it is going to have to give some back. This theory seems to be based on the notion that a slot machine full of coins is like a human being who has drunk several gallons of water and must then "relieve the pressure."

Slots don't work that way. It has no way to sense its coin box, or "stomach," is full so it must disgorge coins or explode. If a machine did get too full, it would stop working, but most casinos service their machines far too regularly for that to happen. And in any case, more and more people are playing by feeding the machine bills and playing with credits rather than handling thousands of coins a day.

No, the "too much to drink" theory doesn't work for slots. The only reason they pay off is because of the RNG timing.

"This Machine Is Hot, I'm Staying With It"

The flip side of the previous theory is the "this machine pays off a lot, I'm going to stay with it" theory. This is better than the "overdue" theory, but not by much. A hot machine is just randomly enjoying a hot streak, in the same way you might randomly flip a coin ten times and see it come up heads all ten. Sometimes these things happen.

The reason this is a better theory will be discussed in the next chapter. In a few words, although every slot machine ultimately makes money for the house, some pay back better than others. If you find a slot that's been paying back frequently, there's at least some chance that you've stumbled upon one of the better machines in the casino.

All Is Not Lost

All of this talk about not being able to change what happens on a machine might sound like you should just give up hope now. That's not true. There most definitely *are* strategies and tricks that can improve your chances of winning. They just don't center around how you jiggle the handle or otherwise physically approach the machine. Good strategies involve selecting the right kind of machine in the right location, as well as, in some cases, knowing how to play the machine optimally. They'll be discussed throughout the book.

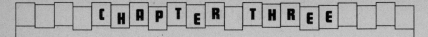

CHAPTER THREE

Speed Kills: What the House Percentage Means

Everyone has heard about house percentages, but few people understand what they mean. You need to understand the house edge in order to select an appropriate bankroll and estimate how different playing styles will impact your expected results.

If you've ever been to Las Vegas, you've probably seen the signs: "Loose Slots," "98 Percent Return," or "Liberal Slots."

Everyone understands that casinos are in business to make money, and that they wouldn't put slots onto the casino floors unless they did just that. It's pretty simple to see that, on the whole, slot machines take in more money than they pay out. Everyone just hopes that the other guy's money goes in and they get the money that comes out.

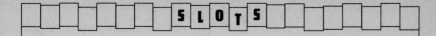

Just how much money goes in and stays in is determined, over the long haul, by the RNGs discussed in the last chapter. When a casino orders a particular slot machine, it can usually order it with an RNG set to return a precise percentage. "Send us a *Red, White & Blue* that returns 92 percent" goes the order, and that's the machine that gets delivered.

What does 92 percent return mean? At one level, it seems simple: Over the long run, for every dollar (or four quarters, or 20 nickels) that gets put into the machine, the machine will pay back 92 cents to customers.

The Long Run Is Very Long

The two most important words in the sentence above are *long run*. In the short run, almost anything can happen. You can put in 20 nickels, one at a time, and lose every single time. You can put in 20 nickels, one at a time, and win every single time. Long run percentages are *long*. Sometimes it takes a machine months or even years before its percentage conforms to expectations.

It is important to understand that a machine has no way of "knowing" whether or not it is conforming to its programmed expectations. In other words, a 92-percent-return machine has no way to recognize that it's been paying back 95 percent and now must start paying less to even things

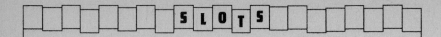

out. If it's been paying low, even as low as 85 percent, the machine will remain oblivious to that as well. It can't hit a reset button of any kind to start paying back more.

This is important because there are players who, thinking they've discovered a "system," get the bright idea to find out which machines have been paying back below expectations. Their reasoning, obviously, is that these machines are now "due." Bad idea. This reasoning is similar to someone who takes a nice, shiny, freshly minted quarter, flips it 20 times, and, after seeing it come up heads 15 times and tails 5 times, tries to take the quarter around to her friends to bet that the coin, when flipped, will come up tails, because she knows the coin is "overdue." In fact, the odds that the next flip of the coin will come up either heads or tails remain even—50/50. The record of coin flips in the past is no predictor of what the record will be in the future. You can't depend on some mythical "law of averages" to help you beat the system.

So, if you can't count on the law of averages to even everything out for you, what should you expect from a weekend playing a 92 percent slot machine? If you bring $300 to gamble with, should you expect, with average luck, to lose $24 by the end of the weekend?

No, you shouldn't. This is one of the most important concepts in this book—maybe even *the* most important. If

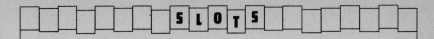

you bring $300 to play the slots, you are *not* gambling $300—that's just the amount of money you happen to have in your wallet.

How Much Are You Gambling When You Play?

There are a handful of factors that come together to answer this question. How much you are gambling is strictly a function of

- What denomination machine you are playing (that is, a quarter machine or a dollar machine)

- How many coins you play each time you spin

- How many times you spin the reels each hour

- How many hours you play the slots in the course of your trip

In plain language, if you play a dollar slot, playing three coins each spin, and you spin the reels 200 times an hour, you are putting $600 into that machine every hour. If you play ten hours a day, for two days, you are putting $12,000 into that machine.

"Hold the phone," you're probably saying. "I've played dollar slots like that, and I certainly didn't bring $12,000 with me. There must be something wrong with those numbers."

Nothing is wrong with the numbers. They all add up. Let's take a look at what's really happening here. The first fact you need to consider is that you win on a lot of pulls, and sometimes you win quite a bit. So money goes in, and then it comes back out again. When that happens, you have a chance to reinvest, or recycle, your winnings. And if you're like most slot players, that's exactly what you do.

Recycled Money Is Like Compound Interest for the Casino

So let's plug in those numbers. You bring $300 to play, and you start playing that dollar slot with the 92 percent return at three bucks a shot. With that amount of money, you can obviously afford to pull the handle 100 times. With average luck after 100 pulls, you'd be down about $24, or 8 percent of your beginning payroll. As we've seen, it's extremely unlikely that you'd be down exactly $24, but it's a useful figure to learn how recycled slot money works. After 100 pulls and an 8 percent loss, you'd have $276 left. With that, you could pull the handle 92 more times, at which point, again with average luck, you'd have lost roughly another $22. Now you're left with $254, enough to pull the handle about another 84 times, and so on, and so on.

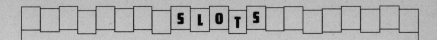

Even though you only brought $300 with you at the beginning of your trip, you're giving the casino much more than $300 worth of action. Because you win on many of your spins, the same money gets to go through the machine many times.

It's important that you remember your actual results won't look precisely like this. Maybe after the first hundred pulls you'll be winning $700. Maybe you hit a cold streak and you're down some cash. In the short run, anything can happen. But the more hours you spend at the machine, the more likely it is that your long-term results will start to resemble what's supposed to happen.

Speed Kills

Because the casino figures to take a small bite out of your bankroll every time they get a shot at it, the faster you play, the faster you'll probably go through your money. Someone who spins the reels 600 times an hour will, all

How Fast Can You Spin?

With the new machines' ability to accept bills for plenty of credit and the Spin Reels button, some players close in on 800 spins in an hour. An average button pusher probably spins the reels about 400 times an hour.

else equal, spend her money about three times as fast as someone who spins the reels 200 times an hour.

As a result, unless you clearly know yourself to be someone who does not enjoy slots unless the reels virtually never stop, one of the smartest things you can do as a slot player is to slow down.

When the reels stop spinning, take a minute to look at the machine you're playing. Use the lever, or arm, occasionally, instead of only the Spin Reels button. Look at the people, take in the atmosphere, talk to a companion. Most people who enjoy slots would have a lot more fun playing eight hours a day at 200 spins an hour than they would playing two hours a day at 800 spins an hour—and their expected mathematical result would be exactly the same.

There's More Than One Way to Skin a Slot

Slowing down certainly reduces the amount of money you put at risk in a weekend of slot play, but there are other techniques you can use to achieve the same result. If you find a 96-percent-return machine instead of one that returns 92 percent, you've immediately cut the house edge in half, from 8 percent to 4 percent. As a result, you can play twice as long on the same money. And you only need to get half as lucky to win! We'll discuss how to find higher return machines in Chapter 6.

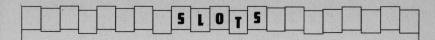
Push or Pull?

Does it matter whether you push the Spin Reels button or pull the lever? Not to the slot machine, but it might to you! Pulling that lever takes more energy than it looks. Switching entirely to the lever can make your arm tired or sore, even though you might not feel it until the next day. You could even get the slot player's version of carpal tunnel syndrome! Use the lever only as a change of pace, unless you know you're in good physical condition.

Another good way to reduce the amount of action you give the casino is to drop down to a machine with a lower denomination. If you're playing a quarter machine, you're only risking 25 percent of the money you'd be risking in a dollar machine. Of course, the rewards for winning also drop when you move to a lower-denomination machine, and for many people, the game isn't as exciting if they're playing a nickel or a penny slot—there just isn't enough to win. The smart move, then, is to play the lowest denomination slot that still excites you. While the point is to minimize the amount of money you have in play, you want to make sure that you don't minimize your enjoyment at the same time.

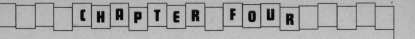
Picking Your Correct Level of Play

Quarter slots don't usually return as high a percentage as dollar slots, but that doesn't mean playing a dollar slot is a wise decision. Similarly, playing maximum lines increases your chances of hitting a jackpot in one weekend, but is it a good long-term idea? Find out how to create the best combination of investment and entertainment.

In the last chapter, we saw that reducing the amount of money you cycle through the slots is a smart way to reduce your risk, cut your potential losses, and improve your chance to win. Unfortunately, people who learn this principle sometimes try to expand and improve upon it, often without the best results.

The idea many people adopt is to play only one coin at a time. Their reasoning makes some sense: If they play three coins in a dollar machine, they're risking three dollars with

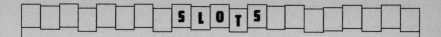

every pull; if they play only one coin, they only risk a dollar. Thus, they figure, they can play much longer with a smaller bankroll.

This is a good example of how a little knowledge can be a dangerous thing. The goal of reducing the amount of money you have in action is sound and smart, of course, so that's not the problem. The problem comes when you try to reach this goal by playing only a single coin. And that is a recipe for a nightmare.

A Rare *Always*

It is not wise to use the word *always* in discussing almost anything, not just gambling. Most principles, no matter how sound, have exceptions and contain gray areas. This situation, however, deserves an *always*. Unless you are playing a pure multiplier machine, you should *always* play the maximum coins in whatever slot machine you're playing. If playing maximum coins means that you have too much money in play, if you decide that three dollars a spin is just too much action for you, you should shift to a lower denomination machine and play maximum coins there.

You are far, far better off, for instance, playing three quarters in a quarter machine than playing one dollar in a dollar machine. Yes, this is true even though the amount of money you have at risk is pretty close and even though dollar machines tend to pay back at a slightly better rate than do quarter machines.

Pure Multiplier Machines Are Rare

Very occasionally you will find a slot machine that offers no incentive beyond increased "action" for playing maximum coins. You don't need to be a slot expert to be able to figure out if you have found such a pure multiplier machine. All you need to do is look at the pay tables printed right on the machine. If the payoffs for additional coins are exact multiples, you've found a pure multiplier machine, and playing one coin is just fine. An example (abbreviated for simplicity's sake) of a pure multiplier pay table would be:

Winning Combination	One Coin	Two Coins	Three Coins
One cherry	2 coins	4 coins	6 coins
Two cherries	5 coins	10 coins	15 coins
Three lemons	10 coins	20 coins	30 coins
Three bars	20 coins	40 coins	60 coins
Three double bars	40 coins	80 coins	120 coins
Three triple bars	60 coins	120 coins	180 coins
Three jackpot symbols	100 coins	200 coins	300 coins

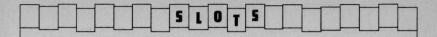
As you can see, there is nothing special to be gained by playing three coins instead of one here. You win three times as much, but you are investing three times as much. How many coins you play on a game like this is strictly a matter of personal preference.

A More Typical Machine

It would be much more common to find a machine with a pay table that looked like this:

Winning Combination	One Coin	Two Coins	Three Coins
One cherry	2 coins	4 coins	6 coins
Two cherries	5 coins	10 coins	15 coins
Three lemons	10 coins	20 coins	30 coins
Three bars	20 coins	40 coins	60 coins
Three double bars	40 coins	80 coins	120 coins
Three triple bars	60 coins	120 coins	180 coins
Three jackpot symbols	100 coins	200 coins	1,000 coins

There is only one difference between this table and the previous one. Now when you hit the big jackpot, instead of just moving from 200 coins to 300 when you shift from two coins to three, you move from 200 coins to 1,000.

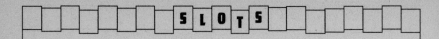

This is an example of a pay table for a nonprogressive machine. The difference when you move to a progressive machine is even more dramatic: Unless you play maximum coins, you do not qualify for the big progressive jackpot.

Try to imagine yourself standing in front of a wide-area progressive slot machine and seeing four jackpot symbols lined up in a row. You gaze up and see that the progressive jackpot is $14 million. Unfortunately, you only played one coin, so your payoff is only $1,000.

Now that's a slot nightmare.

Turning a 92 Percent Machine Into an 85 Percent Machine

By not playing maximum coins in most slots, you lower your effective payback percentage. A big percentage of what the machine gives back to players is in the form of those occasional, wonderful, big-jackpot payoffs. In effect, your decision to play one coin turns a 92 percent machine into an 85 percent machine or perhaps even worse.

The "Buy-a-Pay" Issue

Some machines that *look* like pure multipliers aren't. Although the jackpot doesn't leap with the third coin, some machines, called "Buy-a-pay," will pay off on certain symbols. For instance, the machine might pay off on cherries

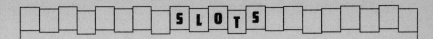

and lemons when you play one coin but pay nothing if you hit three bars. When you play two coins, it would pay double on the same cherry and lemon hits, but it would *also* pay off on three bars. Thus, playing only one coin in Buy-a-pay machines increases the house edge dramatically.

Moral of the story: Unless you are *sure* you are playing a pure multiplier that is not a Buy-a-pay, play the maximum coins on your slot machine!

Don't Confuse Maximum Coins With Maximum Lines

Although playing maximum coins is clearly important on the vast majority of machines, it makes no difference at all how many lines you choose to play. Some machines offer one pay line, some offer three, some five, and some nine.

Deciding how many lines to play is another of those intellectual-versus-emotional issues. Mathematically and financially, it makes no difference whether you play nine pay lines for an hour or one pay line for nine hours. You'll pump the same amount of money into the machine and have the same chance of winning big.

Emotionally, some people have trouble not playing every possible pay line. They might see that if they'd played three lines instead of one, for example, they would've hit a jackpot on the third pay line. Intellectually, getting upset about

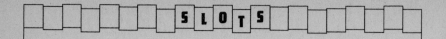

this is the equivalent of getting upset because you only played a machine for an hour when you just knew that if you had played for three hours, you would have hit a jackpot. But, for many people, there is something upsetting about seeing the jackpot that you could have hit but didn't.

Your Maximum Line Choices

If, for purely psychological reasons, you want to go ahead and play the maximum number of lines, by all means do so. But understand that, especially on the newer games offering up to nine lines, you are putting a *lot* more money into play each hour than you would on fewer lines. Once you recognize that, you have three rational choices:

1. You can choose to play fewer hours each day.

2. You can choose to drop down to a lower denomination machine (such as playing five lines on a nickel machine instead of one line on a quarter machine).

3. You can accept the fact that you are putting a lot more money at risk.

Only you know which of these approaches is best for you. Only you understand yourself and your budget. But it is important that you see there is a choice and make a selection that's right for you.

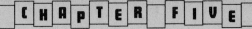

CHAPTER FIVE

Slot Clubs: Getting the Most for Your Money

Just like high rollers, slot players can earn freebies by joining a casino's slot club. There are almost no draw-backs to joining slot clubs and many advantages.

many years ago, table games ruled casinos, generating the vast majority of the profits. Las Vegas was built around high rollers, and high rollers got everything—their room, their airfare, their meals—for free. Slot machines were accommodations placed in casinos to keep the Big Player's girlfriend occupied while he was losing a fortune.

Gradually, Vegas started to change: fewer high rollers, more middle-class gamblers who also wanted freebies (also called "comps" because they're complimentary), and more slot machines. The middle-class gamblers generally didn't get free airfare, but if they gave the casino enough action, they could get RFB (room, food, and beverage) comps. Slot players, however, were still mostly left out in the cold when it came to comps. Casinos still didn't think of slot players as gamblers who gave them enough action to warrant comps, and even if they did, there wasn't any reliable, cost-efficient way to track the amount of action the slot players were actually giving. Casinos gave comps only to players who they thought earned them.

The evolution of Las Vegas and other casino cities into slot-dominated destinations, along with modern technology, has changed all that.

The Credit Card That Gives You Credit

Today, casinos can easily track the action a slot player gives them—more easily, actually, than they can track a table player's action. Tracking your table action has to be done by an employee who eyeballs your bet size from time to time in order to estimate your average action.

For casinos to track slot-machine action, slot players can simply join the casino's slot club, receive a credit-card-shaped plastic card, and insert that card into whatever machine they are playing. The card's magnetic stripe allows the casino to know to the penny how much action slot players have given them. There's no need for anyone to guess whether you're a 200-spin-an-hour player or a 400-spin-an-hour player. There's no need for an employee to wonder if you always play the dollar machines or if you sneak off to play the quarter machines when that employee isn't looking.

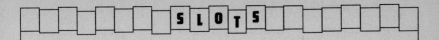

The card gives the casino a precise count, and so the casino can, and will, give you *exactly* the amount of comp credit to which your level of play entitles you.

Joining Is Easy

Joining a casino's slot club and receiving the card is simple. All casinos have a booth or desk where you fill out a form to get your card immediately. Aside from obvious information like name and address, these forms usually ask some marketing questions; whether you answer is up to you. The form also usually asks if you want to receive promotional mailings from the casino. Again, your answer is up to you.

Forgetting your card and accidentally leaving it in a machine is easy to do and fairly common. But don't worry, it's no big deal if you do lose it. The casino will gladly issue you another one for free. It's still an annoyance, though, and this is why you'll see some people attach their cards to their wrists with elastic cords provided free by the casinos.

All Slot Clubs Are Not Created Equal

Different casinos have different ideas about how much your play is worth to them. As with many decisions made in casinos, the ultimate question about the type or amount of comps and credits to give for slot play comes down to a marketing decision: "How much do we have to give away

What If I Lose My Card?

Unlike a credit card, you definitely do *not* have to worry about someone picking up your card and using it. If they do, *you* will get the credit for their play! In fact, some people deliberately leave their cards in a machine, hoping for this to happen.

to stay competitive with our competitors?" As a result, a casino with no competition for 200 miles in any direction might not have a slot club at all, or if it does, it isn't likely to offer as many rewards as an Atlantic City or Las Vegas casino. The more vigorously a casino has to compete with local competition, the more likely it is that its slot club will offer good benefits.

What Kinds of Comps Should You Expect?

Most slot clubs offer from one to three kinds of benefits. Some merely allow you to accumulate points to trade in for merchandise. While this is better than having no slot club at all, you can do better. Others give you actual cash back: X number of points entitles you to Y number of dollars.

Usually, the amount of cash back is a straight percentage of the total amount of money you have put into machines. It's no surprise that the amount of this percentage varies

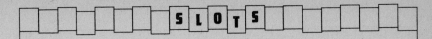

from casino to casino, and unless you subscribe to a newsletter like Anthony Curtis's *Las Vegas Advisor,* you'll just have to do a little legwork to investigate which casinos offer the best deals. Some casinos offer you a choice between merchandise, cash back, and the more traditional comps like free rooms, food, and beverages. All of this is assuming, of course, that you give the casino enough play.

Smart Slot Club Strategy

With the exception of a casino chain like Harrah's, which allows you to accumulate slot club points from any Harrah's casino toward one account, you need to concentrate your play in one casino to get maximum value from slot club memberships. It's OK—indeed, it's a good idea—to join slot clubs everywhere you go, just in case you spend some time playing there, but you'll usually earn significant comps only if you play a lot in one place.

One important thing to find out about any casino's club is whether or not you are allowed to accumulate points between visits. That is, if you come for two days, play a little, and then leave, do your accumulated points stay in your account like frequent flier miles? Or does your account revert to zero at the end of your stay, which would mean that, if you don't give them a lot of action in a short period, you're wasting your time putting the card in the slot?

Your Winning Result Makes No Difference

As with table comps, winning or losing is irrelevant to earning slot club points. Rewards are strictly a factor of how much money you put into a machine. But you have to play. Feeding in a hundred dollars and then pressing the "Cash Out" button won't earn you any club points!

Slot clubs that allow you to accumulate points are, all else equal, better than clubs that don't. But some clubs that do not allow point accumulation may still have nice benefits. If a casino that doesn't allow point accumulation pays, for example, more cash back than the other casinos in the area, you should join and participate when you visit.

The Bottom Line

Slot clubs take some of the casino's edge and give it back to you, much as comps do for table game players, so they're definitely worth your attention. But don't lose sight of the big picture. A good slot club in a casino where you don't enjoy the atmosphere doesn't do you much good if you're playing for enjoyment. Similarly, a good club in a casino filled with low-paying slots doesn't do you much good, either. Clubs are a nice piece of the puzzle, but your overall decision on where to play has to rest on other factors.

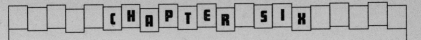

CHAPTER SIX

How to Find the Best Slot Machines

Like everything else in life, some slot machines are good and some are not so good. Learning how to recognize the characteristics that set the payoffs of one slot machine apart from another can provide the difference between a positive slot-playing experience and a more disappointing one.

Like the fountain of youth, the perfect slot machine is more myth than reality. Casinos can't fill their floors with machines that pay back 102 percent and stay in business very long.

In one sense, a better title for this chapter might be "How to Find and Avoid the Worst-Paying Slot Machines," but it's probably better to stick to more positive-sounding advice. Just remember, in this context, when the word *better* is used, it means "not as favorable to the house."

The Three Keys to Find Better Machines

The quest for the perfect slot breaks down into three parts:

1. Finding the best city to play slots

2. Finding the best casino within that city

3. Finding the best machines within that casino

Finding the best city is pretty simple. A fundamental rule of business is that when businesses have competition, they have to operate on slimmer margins and offer decent prices and good customer service. So there's a great deal of incentive to offer good-paying slots in a town with a lot of casinos like Las Vegas or Atlantic City. If customers find they always lose at one casino, they'll just walk next door.

By the same reasoning, a casino with no competition for hundreds of miles does not have the same incentive to offer good machines. Such casinos still have competition, but it's far away. If the machines pay back at rates that are too low, however, only those customers who are most desperate to play will come back. Even without local competition against these casinos, a large number of slot players will not return to low-paying slots. They'd rather incur the expense of a trip somewhere else where they'll have a more enjoyable time.

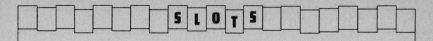

One-Casino Towns Are Like Convenience Stores

It's probably useful to think of playing the machines offered in a one-casino town as the equivalent of shopping at a convenience store. People don't do all their shopping at convenience stores because the prices are higher than at a huge grocery store. But they do sometimes shop at a convenience store because they don't always want to deal with long aisles, hundreds of people, and long lines at the checkout counter. A convenience store is just what it says it is, convenient, and most people are willing to pay a certain amount for that convenience.

If you have to choose between playing 85-percent-return slots at a local casino or 92-percent-return slots at a casino where you have to pay for a hotel room and an airplane ticket, it might well make economic sense to play at the

Competition in a One-Casino Town

Don't assume an isolated casino won't ever offer good slots. After all, convenience stores sometimes run sales. If a casino feels that it's competing for your entertainment dollar not just with casinos but with various other kinds of entertainment as well, it might offer good slot machines.

local casino. Convenience is worth paying for, as long as you don't pay too much.

Choosing the Best Casino Within a Given Casino City

Choosing the "best" casino isn't always a purely economic decision. Some of the factors involved are purely subjective. If you love the atmosphere at Casino A, where the slots return 92 percent, and find the atmosphere at Casino B a bit depressing, even though its machines return 95 percent, you will probably enjoy your vacation more by playing at Casino A. Only you know the answer. To some people, the money is the only thing that matters. For

Multiple Slots

Don't play two or more machines at once. You're not only increasing the chance that someone could steal from one tray while you're looking at the other machine, but casinos rarely place two good machines right next to one another, so it's almost guaranteed that you'll be playing at least one bad machine.

others, the totality of the experience is what counts.

Cold, Hard Statistics Are Available

In big casino towns, statistics are available about the overall payback percentages of casinos. If you don't mind doing a little research, checking out publications like *Las Vegas Advisor* or *Casino Player* can pay big dividends, because you can learn exactly who is, on the average, paying out how much for each level of machine. They don't break this information down by individual type of machine, but you can learn what Caesars Palace pays on its dollar machines, what the Rio pays on its quarter machines, and various other information.

Keep Comfort in Mind!

Don't ignore how comfortable the chairs are! If you're spending hours and hours in slot chairs, it's worth paying attention to your comfort level as part of your overall entertainment experience.

If you're not the researching type, you can still apply a little common sense to the equation. Casinos situated in prime locations have lots of features that will attract people, so they don't need to offer slots that pay as well as dumpier casinos in less desirable areas might. If you visit the Mirage, for example, you get to see erupting volcanoes, exotic white tigers, jungle gardens, and other sights. On top of everything else, you're right in the middle of the Strip. But if you visit a property that doesn't offer all those amenities, the casino probably has to do something to bring people in the door. One of the things it can offer is better games.

Don't Carry This Logic Too Far

You should certainly not draw any absolute conclusions from this like "the slots at any dumpy, out-of-the-way casino pay better than the slots at the Mirage." That's taking the logic too far. There are plenty of dumpy, out-of-the-way casinos that feature slot machines paying considerably less than those at the Mirage.

Cold Slot Machines!

Don't play a machine anywhere you might be considered a "captive audience." Machines near show lines or lines waiting for the buffet get lots of play from people who have nothing else to do while waiting, so casinos can place inferior machines in these locations.

Remember, Las Vegas has so much competition that white tigers alone just aren't enough. There are plenty of beautifully themed casinos in town, and if the Mirage wants to compete with them, it can't offer bad machines. This is one more factor that you should keep in mind when choosing a casino that's right for you.

How to Find the Best Machines Within a Given Casino

This is a hotly debated topic. There are a lot of conflicting theories about where "good" and "bad" machines are placed. Let's start with a few points that are not in dispute.

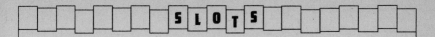

First, higher denomination machines tend to pay back at slightly better percentages than do lower denomination slots. In a casino where dollar machines pay 94 percent, quarter machines probably pay 92 percent or 92.5 percent. It's good to know this, but don't get carried away. It's still better to play three coins for 75 cents in a quarter machine than only one coin for a dollar in a dollar machine. If the amount of money you can win or lose in a quarter game is enough for you, it's silly to quadruple the money at risk just to decrease the house edge by 1.5 percent.

Second, if a slot looks expensive to build and put on the floor, it probably doesn't pay back very well. For example, one of those super, giant-size machines that's eight feet tall with a lever about six feet long not only costs more to build than a smaller slot, it takes up floor space the casino could fill with several smaller machines. Further, the reels tend to spin more slowly on giant machines, which means the casino can't get as many plays per hour. The casino must recapture that lost money somehow, and it does so by making these novelty machines pay back at lower rates.

Some Theories That Aren't Quite So Clear Cut

If you were designing a casino floor layout, would you put the highest paying machines far off in a corner in the back,

where they wouldn't get played as often, or would you put them near the entrance to the slot area, where a jackpot serves as advertising to potential customers walking by?

The "advertising" theory has a lot of adherents, and it makes some sense. If the casino has to pay out jackpots, it might as well get some advertising benefit, and if a machine is off in a corner somewhere, fewer people will see it.

But it's easy to envision a manager taking the opposite approach, and that's one key: Slot managers are human, and humans don't always agree. You should be wary of any absolute conclusions about where the best slots are likely to be. The theory may hold at one casino and be wrong at another.

Casinos That Make Enticing Promises

It is clear that a few of the machines at some casinos are much better than others. The sign for such a casino is... its sign. If a casino's billboard proudly proclaims "98+ percent return slots," you can be sure of two things:

- There are *some* slots that return 98+ percent, because the gaming commission wouldn't let the casino advertise this way if it weren't true.

- There are also some, possibly many, slots that return a much smaller percentage than that.

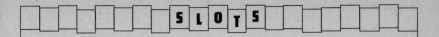
S L O T S

Because no casino anywhere can fill its floor with slots returning 98+ percent and make a profit, the casino's over-all average return will obviously be less. For purposes of this example, let's say that the overall return is 95 percent, although it could even be much less than that. It thus becomes a mathematical certainty that the casino will offer some slots that pay at less than 95 percent, in order to balance out the 98+ percent machines and bring the house average down to 95 percent.

Therefore, any casino that advertises some very high-return slots is a casino where it's worth trying to figure out which machines are better than others.

Simple Observation Helps

You can have all the pet theories you want, and probably none of them is as good as the evidence your own eyes offer you. If you see a machine that hits consistently, it is probably a decent machine.

Because five minutes of evidence really isn't much to go on, and because watching others play for hours isn't much fun for most people, your most useful observations will come from machines you play yourself. If you're doing well, you've probably found a decent machine. If you're getting clobbered, it's probably right to make a mental note about that machine and move on to another.

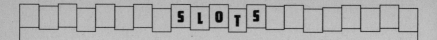

Do Casinos Play a Shell Game With Machines?

Many slot players think casinos move machines around or swap RNG chips so that players can't figure out where the good machines are. A variation on this theory is that the machines lower the return percentage on weekends. These theories are almost always wrong, for a few reasons.

First, remember again that even a "good" machine makes money for the casino. There's no need to hide it.

Second, few players memorize good slot locations. Even if they did, it would take time to gather the information.

Third, the machines are heavy, delicate devices that, all else equal, the casino would rather not be carting around.

Fourth, most casinos don't close, so you'd see it happen.

Fifth, RNG chips are very expensive. Casinos don't keep two or three different chips lying around for each machine.

If your experience tells you that you get worse results on the weekends, don't assume the casino is doing anything sneaky. There are perfectly logical reasons that this may be happening. Casinos are busier on the weekends, so there aren't as many open machines. Also, there are a lot of weekend regulars who have favorite machines. As a result, the machines that tend to be open are probably the less desirable machines. Nothing sinister is going on. It's just that many of the better machines are already in use.

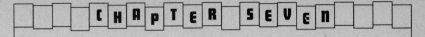
Cautious in the Casino

Although casinos almost never cheat their visitors, casino patrons still have to be careful because crooks, con artists, and swindlers stroll through casinos all the time. Here are a few of the more common scams and ways to avoid them.

F ew places have more distracted people wandering around with lots of cash than do casinos. Beautiful, scantily clad women deliver drinks; dazzling light shows, humming buzzers, and bells add a hypnotic effect. If that's not enough, most players aren't staying in the moment anyway, thinking of money they're winning or losing or dreaming about a huge win.

The combination of distraction and cash attracts a certain criminal element. Casinos understand this and try to protect their customers by barring known thieves and con artists and by providing constant surveillance and plenty of floor security. But you can't depend on the casino to protect you. You need to protect yourself, too.

Beware the Double Team

Anytime anyone asks you anything—if you want a light, if you dropped a coin, will you watch his machine, don't you just love the casino, *anything*—triple your caution level. While your new friend may be just that, casino criminals often work in pairs, using one person to distract the target while the other steals a purse, a wallet, or coins from a tray.

You're Not a Change Booth!

If you're asked to change money or buy or sell coins, put your hand on your wallet and politely decline. The questioner might be setting you up with a distraction or planning to hustle you on the monetary exchange.

Don't Ask for Trouble

Part of the allure of casino visits can be "putting on the Ritz," but you're asking for trouble if you wear lots of expensive jewelry. You make not only your jewelry a target, but your wallet or your purse, too.

You should also keep your money somewhere that's hard to access. For men, your front pocket is much harder to pick than your back pocket or your jacket pocket. For women, it's important to keep your purse closed but also to keep its opening in sight. Don't set your purse or wallet down anywhere, either. It could vanish very quickly.

Seal Those Pockets!

If you own a garment that has pockets that seal with a hook-and-loop-fabric fastener, you might want to use it in the casino. Even if someone crashes into you, it's hard for that person to open a sealed pocket.

Other useful ideas are a money belt or a wallet that loops over your regular belt and can't be removed without removing the belt itself. The more you prepare against pickpockets and thieves, the less attention you'll have to pay to protecting yourself while playing.

Resting Easy in the Rest Room?

If you hang your purse or jacket on the door hook in the stall, you're vulnerable to having someone reach over the door and grab it. It'll take you at least a few moments to clothe yourself and start pursuit, and those few moments are all a thief needs to get away.

Don't Be a Good Neighbor

It's too bad our society has come to this, but if someone asks you to hold something or to watch a machine for him (especially if money is in the tray), politely decline. Most of the time, 99 percent even, the request will be genuine. In the other 1 percent of the times, however, you'll soon wonder where the wallet in your jacket pocket went or where the money in your tray went.

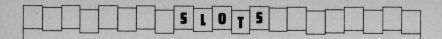

It's also possible that someone who asks you to watch his machine while he's in the rest room is just setting you up for the same request. You've guarded his money, so when the call of nature summons you, it seems obvious to ask for a return favor. Don't ever leave a machine with credits or money in the tray to be guarded by a stranger.

Small-Time Hustles

Not every hustler wants your whole wallet. Some are just lowlifes angling for a tip. Someone who claims he can tell you about a good machine, "and you don't have to give me a thing now, just give me something when you win," is taking a free shot at you. If the machine happens to pay off early, your advisor is sitting there with his hand out. If it doesn't pay off early, your advisor will depart.

Casino employees sometimes do this, too. Sometimes the people who walk around making change might recommend a certain machine. Even if this advice is based on a genuine belief, it's still an angle, still a hustle if the employee takes the initiative in offering you this advice.

If you decide you want to ask a friendly change person about good machines and the advice she gives seems genuine, you can consider tipping if the machine pays off. But the odds are that the change person really doesn't know anything and is simply letting you hustle yourself. You

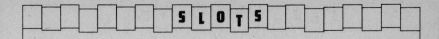

should certainly tip for good service, but anything else and you're probably giving money away for nothing.

Hustlers Outside the Casino

If thieves and con artists are willing to operate inside a casino where there is plenty of security, it stands to reason they will be even more brazen outside. Consider using the valet at all times. If you've stored something so valuable in your car that you're worried the valet might take it, your obvious solution is to get that valuable object out of your car. There's no point in making yourself a target.

Another kind of hustle is selling bad information. If you receive an unsolicited letter or e-mail offering a "secret" system to beat the casino, 99.99 percent of the time that system is worthless. Hustlers know that gamblers want something for nothing, tending to hope more than think. Some gamblers can be easy marks for such hustlers, but you don't need to be one of them.

Beware Unsolicited E-Mail

Mass e-mails cost almost nothing to send, and no matter how good a system is, no matter how impressive its pedigree, it's almost certainly worthless. If the author or sender of the e-mail actually had something valuable to sell, he would be using that information himself or he would publish it through more traditional means.

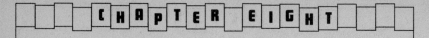
"Session" Play and the Myth of Money Management

Can you identify the classic mistakes and the best psychological techniques of managing your slot money? You will after reading this! There are also some surprising reasons about how good record keeping can save you a lot of money!

Whether or not "Money Management" is a valid gaming strategy is a hotly debated topic among gambling experts. It shouldn't be. The loud debates occur because the experts define the term *money management* differently.

Although proper money management has a place in a gambler's arsenal, it's easy to sympathize with those who proclaim it meaningless. The plausible-sounding management concepts that make up about 90 percent of the "valuable systems" sold to a gullible public are themselves

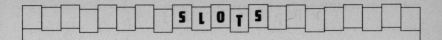

completely meaningless. Much information given the name "money management" provides no useful ideas to help in the casino. If you err on one side of the argument or the other, be someone who believes money management is irrelevant.

Life Is One Long Session

From a purely mathematical viewpoint, quitting while ahead or once you've lost a certain sum makes no difference in your expected results, especially in slots, where emotional control isn't critical. Poker players, on the other hand, can benefit from advice like this, because most find their game deteriorates once they lose a certain amount.

A slot machine doesn't know who's pulling its handle or when it's being pulled. Your likely results are no different if, in the course of a weekend, you play 32 half-hour sessions, 16 one-hour sessions, eight two-hour sessions, or two eight-hour sessions. You're still playing for 16 hours, no matter how you split up the time.

Similarly, if you plan on regular visits to the casino, it makes no difference to your expected win or loss if you always stop play when you reach a certain total. Over the course of your life, you'll play X number of hours at Y bet-size, and no gyrations about when you start or stop will make any difference whatsoever in your cash expectancy.

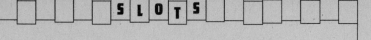
When Math Ends, Personal Psychology Begins

It's critically important that you believe everything you've just read. If you don't, you'll be vulnerable to hustlers selling their worthless money management systems.

That said, proper recreational slot play isn't all about mathematical expectation. If it were, no one would play to begin with, because the mathematical expectation is a loss!

For most people, the enjoyment in playing slots comes from dreaming about winning and experiencing the thrill of seeing a jackpot hit. If you enjoy slots, these positive emotional experiences more than compensate for the times you don't do as well as you'd hoped.

The Value of Stopping to Smell the Roses

Those moments when you hit a big jackpot are wonderful. You feel wonderful, so why not enjoy it for a while? Cash in your winnings, and take the opportunity to walk around feeling like a winner. Go to a show, go eat a nice meal, go do anything that allows you to bask in the good feeling.

Stopping play like this has nothing to do with your life-long expectation of winning or losing, but it has a lot to do with how much fun you have during a lifetime of playing slots. You'll find it easier to focus on the positive feelings if you're not busily pumping quarters into a machine.

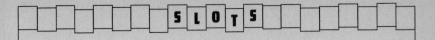

The Importance of Quitting When Losing Badly

Mathematically, quitting when behind won't change long-term results any more than does quitting when ahead. But again, there are nonmathematical reasons to consider it.

The most important reason to quit when your luck goes cold is probably that, at these moments, you're vulnerable to what poker players call "going on tilt," or acting irrationally. A slot player's game can't deteriorate like a poker player's can, but a slot player who's down farther than expected might be in a position to make unwise decisions. For instance, she might try to win everything back quickly and switch to a higher denomination machine, say a $5 slot, that she never would have considered under normal circumstances.

Another important reason to quit when on a cold streak is to stick to your trip budget. You might have decided before the trip that you have a gambling budget of $1,500 for three days. If you decide to break your $1,500 down into three days at $500 a day and then you stick to your resolve even if you lose quickly on the first day, you're guaranteed to still be able to play on the last day of your trip. Is that a benefit? It depends on your personality. If quitting at the $500 point means you quit only an hour into your first day's play and you spend the rest of the day miserable because you won't let yourself play anymore, this system probably doesn't serve you very well.

If this system doesn't work for you, you can continue playing, but you should understand that you're risking one of two bad results. First, you might lose your whole $1,500 budget on the first day and have to quit. The other possibility, which isn't any better, is that you might lose your whole $1,500 budget on the first day and then decide that you can actually afford to lose $2,500 after all.

The middle of a cold streak isn't the time to make important money decisions. If you set a loss limit of $1,500 when you were calmly sitting at home before the trip, you probably had good reasons for choosing that number. Sitting in your hotel room suddenly $1,500 down, you can easily come up with many reasons why $1,500 was too low in the first place. But that kind of thinking usually leads to trouble.

Breaking a bankroll down into smaller session amounts, such as $500 for each day of your trip or $250 for before dinner and $250 for after dinner, might be smart. There's no use in pretending that this is anything other than an artificial device intended to keep you from blowing all your money at once and possibly encouraging you to play smaller-denomination machines, but if it works for you, it's worth it. It doesn't give you a better chance to win or give

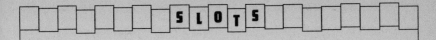

you a smaller chance to lose. It is just one way of managing your money to keep your short-term financial results from falling prey to your short-term emotional results.

You Can't Manage Information You Don't Have

No matter where any given expert stands on the issue of money management, they all agree that if you don't keep some sort of accurate records about your gambling, you're probably winning less or losing more than you think you are.

Kidding yourself about your results is a primary path to a gambling dilemma. It's OK to gamble as a hobby, as long as the amount of entertainment you get is relatively equal to the amount of money it costs you to participate. Lie to your friends if you must, but at least be truthful to yourself.

You might discover your "fun" trips are bleeding off a lot more money than you realized. You might then decide that it would be much more fun to take a trip to Hawaii.

A More Practical Reason to Keep Records

Leaving aside all of the arguments that keeping track of your wins and losses helps you manage your risk better, there is one other excellent reason to keep records: avoiding tax liability.

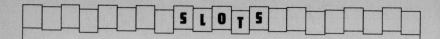

If you hit a big jackpot, you'll have to pay taxes on it just like it's ordinary income. You will be allowed to deduct, from those winnings, any offsetting losses you can prove you experienced in the same tax year.

This is the rule for federal income tax. Some states and municipalities work things a little differently for their taxes, so if you hit for a big number, consider bringing in an accountant or tax specialist to help.

The key word in the deductibility rule is *prove*. The IRS will generally accept a detailed journal if it appears clear that the journal was kept throughout the year and not assembled all at the last moment, and if the entries appear to match your bank balances and expenditures.

Naturally, if you hit a big jackpot in January, this isn't going to be a problem: You know in advance that you should keep records of offsetting losses for the rest of the year. But if you hit for a big number when you're in Vegas over Christmas, there's no time to catch up. If you make it a habit to always keep a record of your gambling winnings and losses, you'll be in a good position to deal with the IRS without getting slammed at tax time.

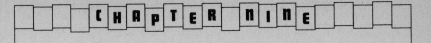

CHAPTER NINE

Slot Machines:
The Next Generation

The slot machines of today have changed considerably from their predecessors. The new machines play differently and offer a different kind of entertainment. Find out what it's all about!

Once upon a time, slot machines were purely mechanical devices that operated with pulleys, levers, and gears. They existed long before electricity was lighting up Las Vegas.

Even for a while after electricity was as widely available as it is today, most casinos resisted installing electric slots. They were not only worried about power failures, they were concerned that electric slots might be easier to cheat. Eventually, though, casinos caught up and joined the 20th century.

Some time after the computer revolution hit, casinos started putting slot machines with the Random Number

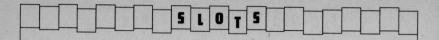

Generator computer chip on their floors, and that opened up a wide range of new kinds of games that could offer much larger payouts to slot players. Still, even after these RNG slots were in use, most slot machines in the casino looked and played much like juiced-up versions of their mechanical ancestors from more than 100 years ago.

Joining the 20th Century in Time for the 21st Century

If you haven't been in a casino for the last decade, though, many of the slot machines you'll see out on the floor today bear little resemblance to the slots you likely saw on your last visit. Although there are still plenty of slots machines with cherries, grapes, oranges, bars, double bars, and triple bars, the world of video has merged with the world of computers to create all kinds of next-generation slot machines.

Some of the new slots are merely video versions of reel slots. These pay back at the same kinds of percentages their reel cousins pay and don't require much discussion. But there are two kinds of slots now available that play very differently from reel machines, and the answers to the questions "Should I play these machines?" and "If I do play these machines, how should I play them?" are not necessarily obvious.

The Next Generation, Part One: Now That's Entertainment

Many of the modern video slots are based on popular themes or television shows. For example, you can now find *I Dream of Jeannie* slots, *The Munsters* slots, and *The Three Stooges* slots. These machines offer the player a much more well-rounded entertainment experience than those at which a player just sits in a chair and hypnotically watches reels spin. Very often, they feature sounds or video clips that offer entertainment even if you are losing.

Because these machines tend to cost a lot to build, take up more floor space than a conventional slot, and get played a bit more slowly than a conventional slot because of the extra entertainment they provide, they also tend to pay back at slightly lower percentages than conventional slots.

There's nothing inherently wrong with this. Slots are supposed to be an entertainment experience, and many players find the new slots infinitely more entertaining than the old variety. Indeed, a whole new generation of players who were never interested in slots before now like and play these machines.

If you do indeed play them more slowly, your expected result doesn't change. For example, if you were to play a 95-percent-return machine at 400 spins per hour, your expected return would be exactly the same as if you played a 90-percent-return machine at 200 spins per hour.

The Next Generation, Part Two: Nine Lines, Anyone?

Because of the computer and video interfaces, another very common feature of next-generation slots is that the player can opt to play as many as nine different pay lines simultaneously. Previously, the maximum was five pay lines, and three was much more common.

You've already learned how vital it is that you play the maximum number of coins when you play most slots. It is almost as vital that you understand the huge difference between playing maximum coins and maximum lines.

Playing maximum coins entitles you to far greater jackpots than if you play one coin. Playing maximum lines entitles you to nothing other than the right to put nine times as

Spotting the Jackpot!

One problem with playing nine lines is that you have to trust the machine to give you your jackpot—many winning combinations aren't always obvious. There's no reason to expect anything other than an honest machine, but most people like to watch as their jackpot lines up rather than be told after the fact that they hit a winning combination.

much money into one machine. This is one reason why nickel slots are making a comeback. Very often, the next generation nickel machines offer you the chance to play up to five coins on each of the nine lines. If you do the math, you see that this nickel slot, played for the maximum, is costing you $2.25 a pull. Some nickel slot!

It is true that, if you only play one line, you will sometimes see a big jackpot on one of the other lines that you would have hit if you had only played more lines. Emotionally, some people have difficulty with this, but it's important to understand that, by playing only one pay line, you can play nine times as long as someone who plays all nine lines!

Mathematically, there is *no* difference whatsoever in your expected return from playing nine lines for one hour than in playing one line for nine hours. Getting upset that you "missed" a jackpot on another line is, logically, no different from getting upset that you might have missed a jackpot by playing for only one hour rather than all day.

Playing maximum coins usually improves your expected return and is a wise strategy. Playing maximum lines, however, is strictly a matter of personal preference. If you find that your slot dollars don't stretch out into as many hours as you'd like, you would probably be wise to stick to one line at a time.

CHAPTER TEN

The Internet: A Source of Play and Information

The Internet brings both virtual slots and an array of gambling information right into your home. This chapter will help separate the wheat from the chaff.

Don't want to drive to the nearest casino? Don't want to fly to a far-off casino? Don't want people to know you like to unwind by playing slot machines? Relax, the Internet is available.

If you've got an online connection, it's easy to start. Find a casino Web site by using a search engine. You might look at several sites before deciding where to play. Most sites require that you download their software to your computer, but some do not.

Once you've chosen a casino, you'll likely see a link or icon for "getting started." That will usually take you to a

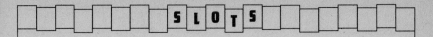

form to join the casino (although some sites require you to download the software first). You'll be asked for your name, address, and valid e-mail address, though some casinos request a little bit more and others a little bit less. If the form asks for more information than you're willing to provide, look for a different casino. At this time, you'll probably also choose a user name and password.

If the site requires a download, you'll do that immediately before or after you register. The casino will provide instructions for downloading and installing the software.

Once the software, if any, has been installed, there's only one more decision to make. Do you want to play for fun or for money? Most online casinos allow both. Some, in fact, suggest that you practice with play money until you've got a feel for how the software works. If you're playing for real money, you'll need to set up an online account with the casino, and the site will provide full information for that. Most online casinos offer a number of ways for you to make a deposit to your account. The fastest way, of course, is to provide your credit card number, but you have other options. Some sites accept transfers from an online bank account, wire transfers, or even personal checks.

Unfortunately, although playing Internet slots certainly provides great convenience, it also presents a few risks. As with almost everything else, it's important to keep your

Be a Doubting Thomas!

You should play doubting Thomas with claims an Internet casino makes. Just because it says it's been operating for three years doesn't mean it's true. It's not that hard to do a little research to find out.

eyes open when venturing into cyberspace. There are potentially costly mistakes out there.

Sending Your Money Offshore

For now and the foreseeable future, Internet gambling is illegal in the United States. Therefore, all Internet casinos are based in other countries. In fact, most are based in small, developing nations that theoretically "license" these operations; in reality, the licenses are just revenue sources for these countries, and not much policing occurs.

Some countries take licensing seriously. Australia and England are two leaders in this regard. Even there, however, it is easier for unscrupulous types to open Internet casinos than brick-and-mortar casinos. (Although riverboat casinos aren't made of brick, the phrase *brick-and-mortar casino* refers to all physical casinos where patrons actually enter, buy physical chips, and sit down to play.)

When you send your money to unknown figures in another country, at least some risk exists that you are dealing with thieves who have no intention of returning it. You can reduce this risk dramatically by dealing with Internet casinos that have been established for several years or that are backed by people of substantial means and reputation.

Crooked Software

One of the best lines demonstrating the risks of Internet gambling is: "The first rule of playing craps is not to play with anyone who is using invisible dice."

When you play Internet slots, you are essentially playing with invisible dice. There's no casino commission guarding your rights. You have no way of know-

What's in a Name?

Many Internet casinos sport names suspiciously similar to famous brick-and-mortar casinos, leading at least some players to think the online casino is associated with the more famous casino. Although the time is not far off when brick-and-mortar casinos will decide to venture into the Internet, that time is not yet here.

ing the kind of payback percentage you're going to get. If the casino sets its software to pay back at 50 percent, it probably won't get a lot of return customers, but the users who have already lost money are out of luck.

Larger, more established Internet casinos are not going to offer 50-percent-return slots. They have spent a lot of time and money establishing their name and position, and they want return business.

Be Careful Out There

A certain percentage of gamblers are problem gamblers who have an addiction not unlike that of cigarette smokers, cocaine users, or heroin addicts. Previously, problem gamblers could avoid most problems by simply deciding not to visit casinos. The presence of Internet gambling removes this barrier. People can gamble away fortunes from the privacy of their own homes.

The private nature of Internet gambling makes it easy for a problem gambler to hide his problem. If someone goes to Las Vegas every weekend, a spouse or friends will notice. But it's easy to conceal Internet casino gambling.

Who Watches the Watchdogs?

Be wary of supposed "industry watchdog" sites. Most of the Web sites claiming to report on Internet casinos that take their time in paying off or don't pay off at all are supported entirely by ads from those very same casinos! How many site managers will have the ethics to blow the whistle on a big advertiser? What's worse, just because you don't see any advertising on a site doesn't mean that the site isn't casino-supported: The support might just be invisible. Although the presence of casino advertising doesn't prove anything is wrong—many prestigious hard-copy publications take casino ads—it is something to watch for.

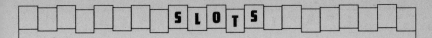

The bottom line: If you have an addictive personality—if you've ever been addicted to anything else—you should think long and hard before gambling online.

The Internet as an Information Source

There's an old saying, "You can't believe everything you read." If that was true of publications you could hold in your hands, it's doubly true of the Internet, where almost anyone can say almost anything.

Just because you read something in an informational Web site or through an e-mail newsletter does *not* mean it is going to be true. On the other hand, there are many sources of reliable information available on the Internet.

Your best bet for information on the Web are sources that also have a presence off the Web, such as the Web sites of respected newspapers and magazines. Among the better Web sites that are currently available for gambling information are www.rgtonline.com, www.casino.com, www.casinoguru.com, and www.vegascorner.com. These sites are currently considered very reliable and feature some of the biggest and best gambling authors on a regular basis. Nonetheless, things can change quickly in the Internet world. If the big names are still there when you visit these sites, they are probably still reliable. But if those big names have departed, be wary.

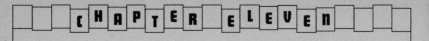

CHAPTER ELEVEN

Video Poker: An Entirely Different Game

Video poker machines might look like slot machines, but they play very differently. If you love regular slots, you may not love video poker, and vice versa. Is it for you?

O ne of the main reasons many recreational gamblers choose slots over table games is their simplicity. There aren't any tough choices to make in slots.

Put the money in, pull the handle, and cross your fingers. It's a simple and comfortable way to relax.

But that attitude at a video poker machine will get you slaughtered. Video poker machines look and sound like slot machines, but that's where the resemblance ends.

Although video poker is simple compared to regular poker—indeed, it actually bears more resemblance to

blackjack than to poker—it is far more complex and diffi-
cult than regular slot play. People who love regular slot play
probably won't enjoy video poker, and vice versa.

How the Game Is Played

There are many different types of video poker machines,
all based on similar concepts. They employ an electronic
52-card deck. At the start of the game, you see five cards.
You then select which cards you want to retain, and after
you have made your selection, you press the "draw cards"
button. The machine then randomly gives you new cards
from among the 47 remaining cards in the deck.

You get paid according to a table printed on the poker
machine, so unlike regular slots, where there is no quick
way to tell if you are playing a good machine or a bad one,
a video poker expert can look at a machine's pay table and
instantly know if the game is worth playing. As an example, a pay table for one version of Jacks-or-Better video
poker might be:

Royal Flush	800 coins	Straight	4
Straight Flush	50	Three of a kind	3
Four of a kind	25	Two pair	2
Full House	9	Pair of jacks or better	1
Flush	6		

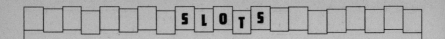

The pay table for another version of the same game might look like this:

Royal Flush	800 coins	Straight	4
Straight Flush	50	Three of a kind	3
Four of a kind	25	Two pair	2
Full House	8	Pair of jacks or better	1
Flush	5		

The only differences in these two pay tables are the payoffs for the full house and the flush. The first machine pays nine and six coins, respectively, for these hands, and the second machine pays eight and five. Experts familiar with the two games know that the first machine pays back at slightly better than 99 percent with perfect play, while the second machine pays back at slightly better than 97 percent with perfect play.

The Key Words Are *With Perfect Play*!!!

Payback figures like 99 percent or 97 percent look awfully enticing. Even better are some video poker machines that actually pay back at slightly *better* than 100 percent with perfect play. When you compare that to most regular slots that pay off at 85 percent to 95 percent, you may ask yourself why you're playing regular slots.

But what exactly does the phrase *perfect play* mean? We don't have room to explain it here, but perfect play is not easy. If you have four cards to a royal flush, such as the K-Q-J-10 of hearts, and your fifth card is the five of hearts, do you break up the guaranteed six-credit win to take a shot at the big money? If you have three of a kind, do you draw two, or hold a kicker?

Your guesses about these answers might be right or wrong, but if you are playing video poker by the guess method, you are most definitely not playing with "perfect play," no matter how smart you are. A few errors here and there can bring your expected return down in a hurry.

A Different Strategy for Every Machine

Depending on the pay table offered, each video poker machine has a uniquely correct basic strategy, so memorizing strategy for one machine doesn't necessarily help on a different machine. Slot players tend to like to play long sessions and to play them fast. At the video poker machine, the faster you play, the more likely you are to make a mistake, and the same goes for playing when you are tired.

Just Say No, Unless...

Unless you enjoy losing quickly, you should stay away from video poker machines until you obtain and memorize the correct basic strategy for any game you want to consider playing. There are many good books available on the subject, and their cost is trivial compared to the cost of playing incorrectly.

> ## Better Than 100 Percent?
>
> Some video poker machines pay better than 100 percent with perfect play, especially when a progressive jackpot builds up to large amounts!

Take the time to read, understand, and memorize a book on video poker. If you're willing to do the work, both before you arrive at the machine and once you are playing the machine, video poker will, without question, give you a better chance of winning than regular slots will.

Like all choices, you have to decide what is right for you. If you enjoy the bells and whistles of regular slots and like the fact that the machine is not too demanding, maybe you're best to stay with the slot machines you're used to. On the other hand, if you've been playing slots but feeling that you'd like a little bit more challenge, perhaps you should give video poker a try.